Crisis Maximus!

Written by Quentin Flynn
Illustrated by Betty Greenhatch

Contents	Page
Chapter 1. *Persistence pays off*	4
Chapter 2. *Wilderness crisis*	17
Chapter 3. *Night-time crisis*	28
Chapter 4. *Entomology expert emerges*	38
Verse	48

ANNAPOLIS ROYAL REGIONAL ACADEMY

NELSON
THOMSON LEARNING

Crisis Maximus!

With these characters ...

Beth

Conrad

Mum

Dad

"I spy with my little eye an

Setting the scene ...

Much to the surprise of Mum, Conrad and Beth, Dad agrees to go on a family camping expedition. But their surprise quickly turns to amusement, as Dad finds himself hilariously out of place in the wilderness. While Conrad and Beth spend their time finding specimens of interesting insects for their entomology club, Dad spends his time stumbling from one crisis to another!

But, just like a caterpillar turns into a butterfly, by the end of the trip, a new Dad emerges — one quite different to their businessman Dad.

insect beginning with 'H'."

Chapter 1.

I don't know how Mum persuaded Dad to leave his world of business for a camping trip. It must have had something to do with the way she had persistently asked him for the past month, and the way she kept dropping hints at every dinner time.

I had to hand it to her — Mum turned craftiness into an artform. She'd always begin innocently enough, asking Dad about his day.

"Shares up and down," he'd mutter, without looking up from the financial pages. "High and low. Work is busy. I'll be working late for the rest of the month."

By now you'd think that Dad would have realised that he had just given Mum all the ammunition that she needed.

"You work too hard," she would say.

"You need to spend less time at work and more time with your family. Let's go away for the school holidays. Camping will be fun!"

Dad would grunt, nod, and rustle the pages of his business newspaper. The idea of Dad going camping was about as likely as his mobile phone not ringing on a Sunday. That idea was not very likely, and very very scary!

"Shares in Chromocorp are up," he would reply, with a smile of satisfaction. "And the shares in Xenocorp are down," he would add gloomily.

Dad worked in a large plush office in the city's tallest building. We were not sure exactly what he did, but it seemed to involve lots of buying and selling of companies, moving money from one bank account to another, and talking in an indecipherable language on his mobile phone at all hours of the day and night.

Dad worked long hours, he always wore a suit, and he rarely went on holiday.

"Buy six million euros," he would shout excitedly into the phone. "Sell ten million Tranzcorp shares," he would whisper secretively. "Get out of dollars," he would add, beaming. "Get into francs."

It was all a mystery to us. But it was Dad's work — his passion, and we understood what that meant. My brother Conrad and I had our own passion: entomology!

Entomology, as we had explained to Dad about fifty times, is the study of insects. Ever since we were young, insects had excited Conrad and I, and all the other kids in our entomology club. We loved beetles, moths, butterflies, dragonflies and just about everything else that had six legs, a head, thorax and abdomen.

"That's nice, Beth," Dad would say, as he vigorously tapped on his laptop and his electronic notebook. "I'm sure entomols are very interesting. It's admirable that you have an interest."

"Dad, they're not entomols, they're insects," Conrad and I would sigh together. But Dad was off in another world.

"Interest!" he would proclaim, and reach for his phone. He jabbed a few numbers and pressed the receiver to his ear excitedly.

"What's the interest rate for US dollars?" he would ask. His eyes would light up, and a thoughtful look would surface. "Buy a hundred thousand. Sell two million yen."

So when Dad *finally* agreed to go on a camping trip, none of us could disguise our astonishment.

"You're right," he had announced to Mum one evening. "I should spend more time with my family. Let's go camping!"

I couldn't imagine what Dad would do while we were in the wilderness looking for rare and unusual insects. I don't think he'd even thought about it much — at least not beyond what business files and equipment he could do without on the trip.

Eventually, the morning of our entomology expedition arrived. Conrad and I had been packed for days. We had our entomology books, our field identification guides, our magnifying glasses, our specimen jars and our outdoor clothes. Everything fitted neatly into two small backpacks.

Dad, we soon discovered, seemed to have a different idea of what needed to be taken on a camping trip. He spent hours packing. Mum stared at the mountain of gigantic suitcases in the hallway. Her mouth dropped open, and a dangerous glint appeared in her eyes.

"What is all this?" she asked, with a perplexed look on her face.

"I'm almost ready," came Dad's voice from the bedroom. Luckily, she couldn't hear him whispering into the mobile phone.

"Sell fifty thousand Protocorp shares," he hissed. "Buy ... ooops, I have to go." He hung up and smiled innocently as Mum poked her head around the bedroom door.

"Yes, yes, almost ready," he repeated, beaming a huge, innocent smile at Mum.

Just then, from behind Mum, Conrad and I erupted into a chorus of grunts and groans. She swung around to observe us heaving a huge cardboard box down the hallway towards the front door.

"And what's that?" grimaced Mum. The heavy cardboard box settled against the hallway table, and the vase of flowers on it wobbled dangerously.

"Gee, Mum!" puffed Conrad. "Are you sure you want to take all of this stuff?" Mum raised her eyebrows suspiciously.

I collapsed on the floor. "It's all from the kitchen," I explained breathlessly, resting against the box.

"The electric frypan, the toaster, the sandwich maker, and the coffee maker," added Conrad. "The microwave's still to come. Dad said you'd want them all."

Maintaining a calm exterior, Mum quickly disappeared into the bedroom, where she found Dad stuffing his clothes, including his neckties, into another suitcase.

"Thank goodness you're here," he said, waving at the bulging suitcase. "Could you sit on my suitcase so I can close it?"

"I don't weigh that much!" Mum said, trying not to laugh. Conrad and I knew this was not a time to interrupt. Sneaking a look at our parents was hilarious enough.

"We're going camping!" Mum said to Dad. "Not moving house!"

Dad glanced at his suitcase. "I'm only taking the essentials," he said, looking most upset.

Mum pulled out a necktie. "And when will you need neckties?" she asked, with a sarcastic tone in her voice.

"Well," Dad started, desperately thinking of a reason. "What ... what if we decide to go to a nice restaurant?" he suggested. He scratched his chin. "Or what if I see an important business colleague on the street?"

Mum sat on the edge of the bed. "We're going camping," she explained patiently. "The children are going to be searching for insects. There will be no restaurants. There will be no business colleagues. There will be no streets. In fact, there will be no other people nearby."

Much to our amusement, we watched Dad look at the ceiling in search of another reason. "But ...," he started.

"And there won't be any electricity," Mum continued in a voice that was growing less and less patient. "So, you see, there's no point in packing the electric frypan or the toaster or even the coffee maker!"

"But ... please," pleaded Dad.

"No buts!" said Mum forcefully. "Now, I want you to repack practical clothing in ONE suitcase only, and close it yourself!"

Dad wisely surrendered and agonised over what to pack, while we returned all the kitchen appliances to the kitchen. Then we placed our three backpacks and the tent in the four-wheel drive.

Finally, just as we were about to hurry Dad along, he appeared in the garage with his suitcase and a sulky look on his face. The suitcase was still bulging, and something that looked suspiciously like a tie was hanging out one side. But at least there was only one suitcase.

"OK," he said, trying to cheer himself up. "Let's go and get some entomols. Is it far?"

Mum, Conrad and I looked furtively at each other as we suppressed our urges to laugh. Dad was trying his best to behave normal, and we did appreciate that. But, somehow, we all knew this entomology expedition would be very different to all our previous ones.

Chapter 2.

After driving for an hour, the city's skyline was fading as farmland stretched out ahead of us.

Conrad and I played 'I Spy' as we imagined what insects we could see in the bushes that streaked by.

"I spy with my little eye an insect beginning with 'H'," said Conrad excitedly. "Here's a clue. They're supposed to live in this part of the country!"

"Umm," I said, pretending I was thinking hard. "A *Hypolimnas bolina*!" I'd never seen a blue moon butterfly before. "I spy with my little eye something beginning with 'P'."

"Hmmm," said Conrad. "*Pericoptus* — better known as a scarab beetle! Cool."

All of a sudden, our four-wheel drive shuddered to a stop. Conrad and I were jolted back to reality.

"What's up, Dad?" I called from the back.

"There's no more road," responded Dad.

"No, dear," said Mum. "We still have another thirty kilometres to go." She pointed to a spot on the map.

Thankfully Mum was the navigator because Dad just looked at the map with a puzzled look on his face. He could read graphs, tables and charts in an instant, but a map ...? For Dad, a map was a series of mysterious squiggly lines and dots and symbols that he didn't even care to recognise.

"Well, they forgot to build the rest of the road," he said matter-of-factly.

"No they didn't," replied Mum. "There is no more sealed road. We have to drive along this track." She pointed to a faint dotted line on the map.

Dad looked alarmed. All he could see ahead were some small trees and bushes and a narrow, rocky dirt track, full of potholes and puddles.

"But what about my four-wheel drive?" he squeaked. "It'll get covered in mud and dirt. Where will the carwash be?"

"Four-wheel drives are built especially for rough-road travelling. And, they're allowed to get, and stay, dirty," said Mum patiently.

Dad's four-wheel drive had never been anywhere except on the smooth tar-sealed roads between our home and his office garage. By the look on Dad's face, neither had he!

Mum pointed forward as Conrad and I swallowed our urges to giggle. Reluctantly, Dad pressed the accelerator, and the four-wheel drive crunched and juddered its way along the dirt track. I had only seen Dad look this worried once before, when he had accidentally told someone to buy ten million shares instead of *selling* ten million.

We clumped and thumped and weaved along the dirt track. Dad concentrated hard, trying to avoid the worst potholes and puddles. He winced every time a rock hit the underside of his four-wheel drive, and he pumped his windscreen wiper sprays furiously every time a splash of muddy water hit the windscreen.

Mum hummed along to the music station, which was now sounding crackly. Conrad and I started to jiggle with anticipation. We were getting close to the spot where we would set up camp for the night. This was exciting!

Finally, we arrived. In front of us was a large clearing, with a perfectly flat area where we could set up our tent. Dad rushed out of the four-wheel drive to inspect the damage. He carefully wiped the splotches of mud and dust off the four-wheel drive with his handkerchief. Meanwhile, Conrad, Mum and I unloaded the camping gear.

"Dad and I will set up the tent," said Mum. "You two can start searching for insects."

That was just what we wanted to hear. Conrad and I grabbed our nets and jars and other entomological equipment and raced off.

"Don't go too far," called Mum, as we headed for the edge of the clearing. But we didn't need to. The air was full of flying insects. And the trees and bushes were probably crawling with great specimens. This was excellent!

By the time Dad had studied the instructions for putting up the tent for the fifth time, he was more confused than when he had started. He picked up tent pegs and turned them around and around, looking most mystified.

Luckily, Mum understood the instructions, and she had the tent up in no time. Dad made a silent exit and looked around the clearing anxiously. Whatever he whispered to Mum caused her to laugh.

"There is no bathroom, dear," she pronounced.

"But I can't hold on for much longer," squeaked Dad, with an embarrassed look. Mum pointed at the trees, and Dad scuttled off with his legs close together.

Meanwhile Conrad and I had been having the time of our lives.

"Look," shouted Conrad, pointing to a red and gold butterfly drifting over the clearing. "*Vanessa gonerilla* — a red admiral!"

I was busy probing the leaf litter underneath a tree with a long stick.

"*Gryllus servillei*!" I announced excitedly. A black field cricket stared nonchalantly up at me, and then wriggled itself back into the leaf litter again.

Five minutes later, Dad reappeared from the trees.

"Look, Dad!" I shouted, pointing to a stick insect camouflaged against a tree trunk. "*Clitarchus laeviusculus*!"

"That's great, Beth," called out Dad, trying to appear interested.

"What took you so long, dear?" enquired Mum from inside the tent.

"*Toiletus naturum*," replied Dad. "What is that thing?" he asked me.

"It's a stick insect," I replied.

Dad shuddered. "It looks creepy. Does it bite?"

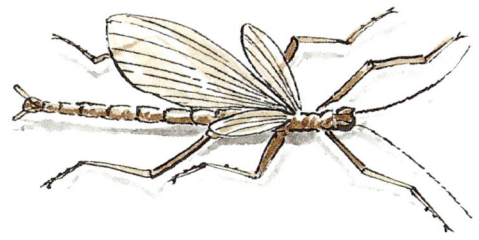

I sighed and smiled at Dad. The only time he felt comfortable around insects was when he was armed with a can of fly spray.

As the sun started to go down, the clouds of insects grew thicker. Fabulous specimens of *Sphinx convolvuli* (sphinx moths) and *Alucita furcatalis* (plume moths) fluttered around the clearing. We were surrounded by the most magnificent-looking moths I had ever seen. Dad sat outside the tent swatting them away with his rolled-up newspaper. He kept looking at his watch and mumbling something about London, New York and Tokyo. Then he casually stood up and strolled innocently towards the trees again.

Conrad and I helped Mum organise the gas cooker. Our thoughts had turned from insects to something far more urgent: dinner! We worked together to get dinner cooking. Soon the smell of sizzling sausages and tomatoes and toast filled the clearing. Somehow, food always smelt even better when it was cooked outside. And, it usually tasted better too!

Just as dinner was almost ready, we heard a shout from the edge of the clearing. We looked up. Dad was running towards us, looking extremely worried.

"Emergency!" he shouted, waving his arms in a panic. In his left hand, he clutched something. "Disaster! I need assistance immediately."

Chapter 3.

Mum looked extremely concerned. "What's happened, dear?" she enquired. "Are you hurt?"

The way Dad was hopping around, I had a dreadful thought that an insect must have bitten him somewhere very painful. That would surely put an end to our expedition!

Dad shook his left hand at Mum. In disbelief, I saw what he was holding. It was his mobile phone.

"No service!" he said in a panic, pointing at the dead screen. "It's a crisis! The phone doesn't work out here."

Mum narrowed her eyes. "Give me the phone," she demanded.

Dad reluctantly handed it over. Mum pressed the 'off' switch. Dad started to chew his fingernails in alarm.

"But ... but ..." stammered Dad.

"Don't worry, dear," said Mum, checking the food. "The rest of the financial world can survive without you until Sunday."

Dad breathed a deep sigh and resolved to pretend he was happy. From the stressed look on his face, he wasn't so sure that the rest of the financial world could survive without his expertise. Then he looked at Mum, Conrad and I.

"Yes, I suppose it will," he said, finally calming down. The tone of his voice still didn't sound like he was entirely convinced. We all realised that, out of his natural work environment, Dad was hopeless!

"Here, have a sausage," offered Conrad. He leant over and passed a freshly-sizzled sausage wrapped up in toast to Dad. Dad cheered up and appeared surprised that we had managed to cook anything out in the country.

"All this wilderness stuff makes you hungry, doesn't it?" he grinned. He devoured his sausage. "Tastes better than the finest dinner in the city," he said, licking his lips.

"Seven o'clock!" he said, as he checked his watch again. "Great! Now I can watch the business report on Channel Ten."

Mum didn't even bother looking up.

"On what, dear?" she asked, winking at Conrad and I. Without thinking, Dad looked around for the remote control that was usually by his side. Then he looked crestfallen. But even he laughed as the rest of us dissolved into a fit of the giggles.

After dinner, we washed up the plates in water we'd collected from a nearby river. Conrad and I hunted through our backpacks for our torches, and shone them up into the cool, dark night air. Away from the city, there seemed to be millions more stars up in the sky.

Noisy moths buzzed and spluttered into the beams of light from our torches. The night was alive with nocturnal insects.

"*Hepialus virescens*," I said, following a large ghost moth with my beam.

"Look, over here!" cried out Conrad. "Wait till we tell all the other kids in the club about that!" He had a fabulous magpie moth, *Nyctemera annulata*, caught in his torch beam. Even Mum and Dad joined in.

"What's that?" asked Mum excitedly, as a black, white and grey moth flew overhead. Its compound eyes glinted in the torchlight. I hurriedly turned the pages of my field guide until I found it.

"*Declana atronivea*," I said, pointing at the photograph and the description. "A black speckled moth. It's rare. What a discovery!"

Dad waved his torch about erratically. Secretly, I think he was less interested in seeing moths than in keeping them well away from his head. He ducked and waved his arms around furiously every time anything bigger than a mosquito zoomed in close.

Finally, it was time to head inside the tent and crawl into our sleeping bags. We were all exhausted. Of course Dad spent ages checking inside his sleeping bag for any extra friendly bugs. Once he was satisfied that he was alone, he settled down.

Feeling cosy, we all huddled together in the tent, making spooky shadows with our torches and fingers on the wall of the tent. This was the most fun we'd had as a family for ages. Even Dad managed to make some clever dollar signs on the tent with his torch and fingers, which was pretty imaginative for him.

It was only when Dad started punching the air and making weird hand-signals that we decided it was time to stop. With four people crammed into a tent, this was no place to re-enact life in the New York stock exchange!

We settled down to sleep. At first light tomorrow morning, we wanted to get up. There were still plenty of insects to be identified, drawn, and written about, around our campsite. And tomorrow would bring some new experiences for Dad too. We all needed to get some rest.

Suddenly, just as we were all about to drift off to sleep, Dad leapt out of his sleeping bag and almost tore the tent down. He was jumping about and slapping his arms and face.

"Bug!" he shouted, and the rest of us just about jumped out of our skins. "A bug crawled into my sleeping bag!"

Conrad scrambled for his torch, and switched it on. Amidst the flashes of yellow torchlights, Dad seemed to be doing some kind of strange dance that involved a lot of stamping and grunting. One glance at the mess under his feet, and I realised that Dad was stamping on a cockroach that had crawled in for a visit.

"Oh, no, Dad," protested Conrad. "It's only a cockroach. *Blatta orientalis*. They're harmless. And fascinating, too."

Dad found his own torch and peered down to look at the crunchy, slimy mess he had stamped on the floor of the tent.

"A cockroach? No, I think you're wrong," he said finally, crawling back into his sleeping bag and closing his eyes. After he placed the financial newspaper over his head, we heard his muffled voice.

"Looks to me like it's a *Deadus flattus.*"

Even Mum had to laugh at Dad's witty joke, even though she knew she shouldn't have.

Chapter 4.

The next day was even better than the first. Conrad and I spent every hour of daylight searching for new and interesting specimens. This was an entomological paradise. Out here, away from the city, every type of beetle, fly, and butterfly seemed to flourish.

Mum helped us collect specimens and recorded their characteristics before letting them go. Fairly soon, we thought we had catalogued just about every six-legged thing that lived around our campsite. Of course, we were wrong. For every insect seen, there are probably about a hundred camouflaged or hiding away somewhere else.

Occasionally, one of us would volunteer to check on Dad, just to make sure he wasn't causing any more trouble.

Whenever there was too much silence around the campsite, we started to get worried. Dad seemed to be an expert at creating a crisis out of nothing!

But even Dad seemed to be getting used to life in the wilderness. As long as he could read his financial newspaper, over and over again, he appeared to be quite content. Once in a while, we would show him a particularly unusual specimen we had found, and he wouldn't even cringe. In fact, he was becoming quite interested in entomology.

As the sun set over the hills that evening, we all sat around, discussing the day's events and drinking hot chocolate. But we still kept our eyes peeled for the next unusual insect to make an appearance.

Suddenly, Conrad spotted a large moth, hovering behind Dad's head.

"Wow!" Conrad exclaimed. "That's unusual!"

I quickly scrabbled around for my field guide but I couldn't find it anywhere. I studied the moth fluttering gracefully.

"Maybe it's a *Helio spectrum*," I suggested. Where was that book?

"No, it looks like a *Hubrium delicans*," said Conrad. "Look at the dotted markings around the edges of its wings."

"*Dasypodia selenophora*," muttered Dad from behind his newspaper.

"Pardon?" said Mum in surprise. Conrad and I diverted our attention to Dad.

Dad dropped his newspaper down to reveal where my field guide had disappeared to. There it was lying open on his lap.

"It's a peacock moth," said Dad, nonchalantly. "While you've been out exploring, I've been doing my own research too," he explained, showing us the relevant page in my field guide. We stared in amazement. Dad was right.

"But ... how did you know that?" I stammered. Conrad looked at Dad as if he had just discovered a brand new species altogether!

Dad grinned and flicked the pages of his old newspaper. "Even I can only read the financial newspaper a few times before I get bored," he said. "And there's nothing else to read around here. And, as you very cruelly made me leave the TV at home, I thought I'd read about entomology. At least then I'd know what I was squashing at night."

I could see that Dad was secretly quite proud of himself. And, the funny thing was, I was quite proud of him, too.

I knew that it had taken a lot of effort for him to read through my field guide. Insects and entomology do not interest everyone — but Dad had done his best to find out something about my passion. Even if he resorted to reading it because he was bored, I still thought that was nice of him.

"Actually," continued Dad, "I've learned that insects are quite interesting. We work with a lot of agricultural companies, and I never realised what a big impact insects can have on agriculture. If there are a lot of insects in one year, they can damage an enormous amount of land and crops. The price for things like coffee, wheat and spices can escalate, just because of a few buzzy beetles in the wrong place at the wrong time. Most interesting."

Even I found Dad's explanation quite interesting. Maybe ... just maybe, Dad and the rest of us could discuss the same things for a change.

By the time we had finished chatting, the moth had flown away. But I didn't mind. There would be plenty more moths to spot later.

Before the sun set, the air was full of clouds of midges and mosquitoes, whining busily overhead. The smell of a whole family of humans was just irresistible to mossies. A huge mosquito landed on Mum's arm, and she slapped it before it started to bite.

"*Culex pervigilans*," piped up Dad, beginning to really show off his new-found knowledge.

I pretended to study the remains of the mosquito on Mum's arm.

"No," I said finally, crawling back to Dad and closing my eyes. "I think you're wrong. Looks to me like it's a *Squishius squashus*."

Everyone laughed. This really was the most excellent, most entertaining, entomological expedition ever!

As the night sky came alive with a full moon and a glittering array of stars, it was a nice feeling.

And what was the best discovery on this trip? Not a six-legged creature with a head, thorax and abdomen — but a two-legged creature with a dead mobile phone, an old newspaper, and a happy grin on his face: *Fatherus humorous*!

"Splat!"

It's peaceful, it's quiet, out here
No TV, no power, no phone
Silence and serenity, all around
Except — what's that buzzing?
Culex pervigilans!?
TAKE THAT!
SPLAT!